RIVERSIDE COUNTY

Nature's Children

TURKEYS

Ben Hoare

GROLIER
EDUCATIONAL

FACTS IN BRIEF

Classification of Turkeys

Class: *Aves* (birds)
Order: *Galliformes* (game birds)
Family: *Meleagrididae* (turkeys)
Genus: *Meleagris*
Species: *Meleagris gallopavo* (wild turkey) and
                  Meleagris ocellata (ocellated turkey)

World distribution. Throughout the United States and northern Mexico. Ocellated turkeys live only on the Yucatán Peninsula.

Habitat. Forests, woods, and nearby fields.

Distinctive physical characteristics. Huge body; strong red legs; chickenlike beak. Naked, warty skin on head and neck. Broad, fanlike tail, and dark, colorful plumage.

Habits. Shy and secretive. Stays close to home and lives in small groups. Roosts in trees at night. Males make loud "gobble, gobble, gobble" calls during the mating season.

Diet. Mainly leaves, seeds, nuts, and berries; also a few insects.

© 1999 Brown Partworks Limited
Printed and bound in U.S.A.
Editor: James Kinchen
Designer: Tim Brown
Reprinted in 2002

Published by:

GROLIER
EDUCATIONAL

Sherman Turnpike, Danbury, Connecticut 06816

Library of Congress Cataloging-in-Publishing Data
Turkeys.
     p. cm. -- (Nature's children. Set 7)
     ISBN 0-7172-5550-6 (alk. paper) -- ISBN 0-7172-5531-X (set)
     1. Turkeys--Juvenile Literature. [1. Turkeys.] I. Grolier Educational (Firm) II. Series.

QL696.G27 T87 2001
598.6'45--dc21

00-067244

Contents

People have kept turkeys for their tasty meat for hundreds of years. Turkeys look a little like chickens, only much bigger and with no feathers on their heads and necks.
Like chickens, turkeys have a reputation for being stupid birds. There are lots of stories about just how stupid turkeys are. One tale says that turkeys can drown themselves by staring up too long at the rain! When something is a failure, we call it a "turkey."

Most of these stories are exaggerations or simply untrue. They are usually about captive birds living on farms and in backyards. Wild turkeys are very different. They have fascinating behavior and are much more intelligent than their farmyard cousins. You may not believe it at first, but wild turkeys are among the most spectacular and interesting birds in the entire United States. Read on to find more about these birds.

Heavyweights

The wild turkey holds the title of heaviest American land bird. Male turkeys usually reach 22 pounds (10 kilograms), but a few grow even larger than this. To give you an idea of how big turkeys are, males weigh 500 times more than most garden songbirds. Female turkeys are only half as heavy as the males, but that's still pretty big.

Being so big creates problems. Turkeys have huge appetites, so they can only live in places where there is lots of food. Flying is hard work, too. It is difficult for turkeys to get into the air and dodge obstacles such as trees. They also need enormous chest muscles to power their wings. It is not surprising that whenever possible, turkeys prefer to walk rather than to fly.

Strange Decoration

Although there are no feathers on the turkey's head, its red and blue markings actually make the head more colorful than the rest of the bird's body. The bare skin is rough and covered with spots and warts. Flaps of baggy skin called wattles hang from the turkey's chin. Adult males have "beards." They are not like the beard's people have, but instead are made up of several of the wattles. Some female turkeys have beards too!

With their colorful, warty skin, turkeys look very ugly to humans. However, we probably look rather strange to a turkey!

Opposite page: *Turkeys are well known for their colorful heads.*

Family Connections

Turkeys belong to a large collection of ground-living birds called the Galliformes. This group also includes chickens, partridges, quails, and pheasants. All of these birds have plump bodies and are very good to eat. For this reason they are popular with hunters and are known as game birds.

Another thing the game birds have in common is powerful legs and long, strong toes. They need them because so much of their life is spent on foot. A wild turkey walks about 2 miles (3.8 kilometers) every day in search of food. It may walk 10,000 miles (16,000 kilometers) in its lifetime—that's like walking half way around the Earth!

Down in the Woods

Forests and woodlands are the wild turkeys' homes. They live in woods all over the United States, apart from much of the Rocky Mountains. Turkeys can also be found in many parts of northern Mexico.

Turkeys from different parts of America are a little different from each other. The turkeys from the west have shorter legs than those that live in the east.

Turkeys don't like dark forests where the trees are close together. A mixture of trees and open places like meadows suits them much better. Turkeys often leave the wood to visit nearby fields of hay and corn. They travel the same way each time, making trails through the undergrowth. But the birds always return to the safety of the woods before nightfall.

Opposite page: *These turkeys have left their home in the woods to look for food in an open meadow.*

Hide and Seek

You might think that a bird as big as a turkey would be bold and fearless. Nothing could be further from the truth. Most wild turkeys are shy and disappear at the slightest noise.
In some places, though, the turkey's homes are quite close to where people live. These turkeys see people all the time and have become more used to them.

A turkey can hear you long before you get close enough to see it because it has excellent hearing. It also knows all the paths through its woods, in the same way that you are familiar with the streets in your neighborhood. That means that it can slip away undetected. Instead of flying, which would take a lot of effort, the turkey just walks quietly away.

Shhhhh! You will have to be very quiet if you want to see a group of turkeys in the wild like this.

Daily Routine

Normally the turkey spends a few hours in the early morning looking for food, and then rests. But the rest time is not spent doing nothing. The turkey takes this opportunity to preen (look after) its feathers, which keeps them in top condition. It also performs a type of behavior called "dusting." When a turkey is dusting, it goes to a patch of dirt and rolls around. It fluffs up its feathers to allow the dust and soil to reach the skin underneath. These antics may look strange to us, but they actually clean the feathers. In the middle of the afternoon it is time for the turkey to begin feeding again. It is very alert and does not stop in the same place for long.

Opposite page: *It takes lots of work to keep feathers looking this good.*

Safe and Sound

When it starts to get dark, each turkey finds somewhere to sleep for the night. It is too dangerous for a turkey to roost (sleep) on the ground. Many hungry animals are out and about at nighttime, looking for a meal. The turkeys walk to a large tree and fly up onto a thick branch. Sometimes several turkeys will sleep near each other or even in the same tree. There they are safe from coyotes, foxes, and bobcats.

Each turkey stays on its perch until daybreak. Then it stretches and ruffles its feathers before jumping down to the ground. It wastes no time in starting to feed.

Scratching a Living

Opposite page:
It can be very difficult for turkeys to find enough food to survive in the winter snow.

In winter a turkey needs to be tough to survive. It ekes out a living by digging through snow to reach buried food. If the bird is lucky, it will find a grassy hollow that a deer has pawed out of the snow. The deer has already done the hard work.

If you walk through fields during winter, you may see the telltale scratch marks left by hungry turkeys. They have been out looking for spilled oats and corn. Usually some grain gets left behind after the harvest. They are a vital lifesaver for a hungry turkey.

In a harsh winter the turkey has to travel much farther to find enough food. The combination of smaller meals and lots of walking is quite a strain. A turkey may lose half of its body weight before spring returns.

Fruits of the Forest

Like other game birds such as chickens, the wild turkey is "omnivorous." This means that it eats both plants and animals. In the summer months the turkey feasts on grass seeds, green shoots, and insects. Its favorite foods are grasshoppers, crickets, and beetles. It snaps them up by stabbing with its bill.

The fall is a time of plenty, with acorns, chestnuts, and beech seeds scattered all over the ground. The turkey also eats lots of fruits and berries. At this time of year the bird puts on weight and soon becomes quite fat. The fat will help it survive when the hard times in winter come around again.

Springtime Squabbles

Early spring is when wild turkeys find a mate. The warmer weather and longer days tell them that the breeding season has finally arrived.

The first thing to happen, as early as February, is that females separate from the males. They gather in their own female-only groups. These groups roost apart from the males, in different trees.

Meanwhile, the male turkeys become more aggressive toward each other. Tempers flare, and fights start to break out. The rivals fly angrily at each other with outspread wings. Male turkeys have horny spurs on their ankles, and they use these weapons to lash out at their opponents. These fights can look vicious, but it is unusual for a turkey to be hurt seriously.

Red in the Face

A male turkey undergoes dramatic changes in spring. His bald head and neck are transformed by big, bright red swellings. The "tube" of baggy skin that sprouts from the turkey's forehead becomes thicker and longer. It swings from side to side as the turkey moves his head. Often it droops right down over his bill, completely hiding it from view. Balloonlike pouches of red skin also grow on the turkey's chest.

Believe it or not, female turkeys find this makeover really attractive. Stronger males change the most and will attract more females than their less colorful rivals.

Opposite page: *If you were a male turkey, you would feel very proud if your head was this red and bumpy!*

Gobble, Gobble, Gobble

At dawn the male wild turkey makes strange
calls that have earned him the nickname of
"gobbler." He goes "gobble-obble-obble-quit-
quit-cut." He also forces air out of his lungs
to make a puffing sound. Then he pushes his
chest out to create a deep, rasping noise.
Another trick is to gradually let the air out
of his chest. This produces a rumbling boom.
Other strange noises include yelps, clucks,
and whistles. The gobbler repeats his bizarre
chorus again and again.

Why does the male turkey gobble?
The simple answer is that it lets females know
he is in the area and ready to mate.
The gobbling calls are so loud that they can
be heard about one and a half miles
(2.4 kilometers) away. They are a very
effective form of advertising.

Some people say that some of a male turkey's calls sound like "turk, turk, turk," which may have helped the turkey get its name.

Strutting Around

When a female arrives on the scene, the gobbler puts on a superb display. He struts to and fro as if very pleased with himself. At the same time, he spreads his long tail feathers into a beautiful fan. As the display reaches its end, the male vibrates these feathers rapidly to make a deep "chump-hum" sound. If the female is impressed, she chooses him by crouching down in front of him. But she may be disappointed, in which case she walks away to listen for another male.

A male turkey does not stop gobbling and displaying once he has mated with one female. He will often keep on until he has mated with several different females. Some female turkeys may also mate with more than one male, too.

Opposite page:
This male turkey is putting on an impressive display. The females do not seem to be very interested, though.

31

Big Families

Female turkeys raise their families on their own. Males offer no help, and they may never even see their babies.

Each female finds a quiet spot to make her nest. Deep grass or among bushes are good places. There she lays a big clutch (batch) of up to 15 eggs. She sits on them to keep them warm for about 28 days.

The eggs usually hatch in late afternoon. The fluffy chicks are called poults. After they have hatched, the poults follow their mother as she searches for food. Poults have many enemies, including raccoons, opossums, skunks, foxes, crows, and snakes. The poults must hurry. There is no time to lose!

Poults are in the greatest danger just after they have hatched. In fact, in the wild most poults will die before they are two weeks old. This may sound very sad; but if every turkey mom had 15 poults that survived, the world would soon be full of nothing but turkeys!

Living Together

It is common for the chicks of several females to stick together. Adult turkeys, too, enjoy company. In fact, if you see one turkey, there are probably several others nearby. This way there are more eyes and ears to look and listen for danger.

Your best chance of seeing wild turkeys is when a flock of them looks for food in a field. The birds stick close to each other for protection. They take turns acting as lookout. One of them always has its head up to watch for enemies while the others are feeding. They then swap positions, so everyone gets a chance to eat.

Opposite page: *A young turkey with one of its parents. During their first month poults double their weight every week!*

Colorful Cousin

Opposite page:
You can see almost every color in the rainbow on this ocellated turkey.

In the tropical rain forests of Central America lives another kind of turkey. It is found only in a remote region called the Yucatán Peninsula, which includes part of southern Mexico, Guatemala, and the northern half of Belize.

This turkey is smaller than the North American wild turkey, but it is far more colorful. Sky blue skin that gleams in the sunlight covers the male's head and neck. Bright orange swellings of skin on the face provide extra decoration. There are also shining spots on the wings. They look like eyes and give the turkey its name—the ocellated turkey. "Ocellated" means a pattern of eyelike shapes.

It may take you a lot of searching and patient waiting before you get to see an ocellated turkey in the wild like this.

Bird of Mystery

In spite of its rainbow colors, the ocellated turkey is difficult to see in the wild. It can usually only be found living in thick rain forest, where it is hard to find. If anything, this turkey is even more shy than its bigger northern relative. But, just as with the wild turkey, some ocellated turkeys that live nearer the edge of the forest have become less wary of people.

The ocellated turkey follows narrow paths through the forest in search of seeds, fallen fruits, and fresh leaves to eat. It also gobbles. But we don't know much else about its habits. Most of its life remains a mystery.

Food Fit for a King

Opposite page:
These turkeys are being bred for their meat on a turkey farm in England. Today, some farms have as many as 25,000 turkeys.

The first wild turkeys were brought from America to Spain in 1519 and to England five years later. They soon became popular at royal banquets. Until the 18th century turkey was only served at the tables of the rich. Today, turkeys are farmed all over the world, and many more people can afford to eat turkey if they want to.

In America it was the early colonists who began the tradition of eating turkey at Thanksgiving. The first settlers ate goose because that was how they celebrated special occasions back in Europe. Turkey soon replaced goose as the main meal, because geese are expensive to raise, and there were lots of wild turkeys to be found in America.

Hunting Target

Turkeys are a favorite target of hunters.
It takes a lot of skill to find the big birds,
which makes the sport exciting. And hunters
can cook their prizes afterward! Roosting
turkeys make the easiest targets, especially if
outlined against a moonlit sky.

But too many turkeys were hunted, and they
became rare. By 1942 there were only 5,000
turkeys in the whole of Mississippi.
Now, turkeys are protected in many states.
People can shoot them only at certain times of
year. Most hunting is in the fall and spring.

People might not have been allowed to
shoot so many of them if the turkey had
become the national symbol of the United
States instead of the bald eagle. This very
nearly happened because Benjamin Franklin
was very eager to have the turkey chosen.
Many people did not like the idea, however,
and so the eagle was picked instead.

Opposite page:
Unfortunately for turkeys, their magnificent feathers and colorful skin make them an easy target for hunters.

Turkey Calling

Opposite page:
If you can learn to copy a turkey's call, you might be able to have a "conversation" with this male.

Once you have heard the wild turkey gobble, it is quite easy to mimic (copy) the distinctive sound. You can even try calling to a real turkey. If you choose the right place at the right time, a male might answer you. He may be fooled into thinking that a rival turkey is in the area. The irritated bird will try to outperform the unwelcome "intruder." It is sometimes possible to make a male turkey leave his hiding place and come into full view. Wild turkey calling has become so popular that contests are held throughout the United States!

The first people to learn to copy the turkey's calls were the Native Americans. They had been keeping and hunting turkeys for their meat long before the first colonists arrived in America.

A Turkey or an India?

You might wonder why a bird that is from America is called a "turkey." No one is sure, but this name was probably given to the bird because people got confused about where the turkey actually came from. The turkey was first brought to England by merchants who came from the Turkish Empire in the Mediterranean. These merchants were called "Turks," and it probably did not take people long to start calling the birds "turkey birds" and then turkeys.

Many people thought the birds came from India. There are two reasons for this. First, the Portuguese took some of the turkeys they found in America to their colonies in India. These turkeys eventually found their way from India to Europe. The second reason is that the Europeans used to call the turkey's home of America the "Spanish Indies" or "New Indies," and this just made people even more confused! In fact, in some languages the word for a turkey can be translated as "bird of India."

Words to Know

Breed To produce young.

Clutch A batch, or group, of eggs that are laid in one nest at around the same time.

Dusting When a bird rolls around in the dirt to keep its feathers in good condition.

Flock A group of birds that feed, rest, and travel together.

Galliformes The group of birds that includes chickens, partridges, quails, and pheasants.

Game bird Wild birds that are good to eat and that people like to hunt.

Mate To come together to produce young.

Mimic To copy.

Ocellated Covered in eyelike patterns.

Omnivorous Describes animals that eat both plants and other animals.

Poult A young turkey.

Preen To clean and repair feathers.

Roost The place where a bird sleeps. When a bird sleeps, we say it is roosting.

Ruffle To shake and "plump up" feathers.

Wattle The flap of baggy skin that hangs from a turkey's chin.

INDEX

Cover Photo: Mike Lane / NHPA
Photo Credits: Stephen Krasemann / NHPA, pages 4, 12, 15, 21, 24, 30; Werner Layer /
Bruce Coleman, page 7; John Shaw / NHPA, page 8; Robert Maier / Bruce Coleman, page 11;
Joe Blossom / NHPA, page 16; Dan Griggs / NHPA, page 19; Mike Lane / NHPA, page 26;
Eric Soder / NHPA, page 29; Hans Reinhard / Bruce Coleman, page 33; Stephen J. Krasemann
/ Bruce Coleman, pages 34, 42; John Cancalosi / Bruce Coleman, page 37; Kevin Schafer /
NHPA, page 38; Bill Coster / NHPA, page 41; Jeff Foott / Bruce Coleman, page 45.